I0605344

Anime and Manga Fan Culture

Bradley Steffens

San Diego, CA

For more information, contact:
ReferencePoint Press, Inc.
PO Box 27779
San Diego, CA 92198
www.ReferencePointPress.com

LIBRARY OF CONGRESS CATALOGING-IN-PUBLICATION DATA

Names: Steffens, Bradley, 1955- author
Title: Anime and manga fan culture / by Bradley Steffens.
Description: San Diego, CA : ReferencePoint Press, 2026. | Includes bibliographical references and index.
Identifiers: LCCN 2025002516 (print) | LCCN 2025002517 (ebook) | ISBN 9781678210687 library binding | ISBN 9781678210694 ebook
Subjects: LCSH: Anime (Motion pictures)--Juvenile literature | Manga (Comic books)--Juvenile literature | Fans (Persons)--Psychology--Juvenile literature | Popular culture--Japanese influences--Juvenile literature | LCGFT: Film criticism | Comics criticism
Classification: LCC NC1766.J3 S73 2026 (print) | LCC NC1766.J3 (ebook) | DDC 791.43/340952--dc23/eng/20250306
LC record available at https://lccn.loc.gov/2025002516
LC ebook record available at https://lccn.loc.gov/2025002517

CONTENTS

A Deep Connection

Ever since a lovable little android named Ambassador Atom zoomed into the hearts of Japanese comic book fans in 1951, Japanese comics, known as manga, and animated films, known as anime, have become a global phenomenon. A 2021 study by researchers at East Texas A&M University estimated that 60 percent of all animated television programs broadcast and streamed worldwide were anime. According to the research firm Ampere Consumer, 2.9 billion people—more than a third of the world's population—watched at least some anime in 2024.

The manga industry is just as large, and possibly larger. According to *Publishers Weekly*, 49 percent of the graphic novels sold in the United States in 2023 were manga. Their popularity is skyrocketing. The 21.8 million copies sold in 2023 were four times the sales in 2020. Grand View Research estimates that worldwide manga sales topped $13.6 billion in 2023.

The numbers tell only part of the story. Captivated by anime and manga's intriguing characters, complex storylines, and universal themes, a diverse and loyal fan community has grown up around the popular Japanese art forms. Anime and manga fans connect online, meet face-to-face, dress up in costumes inspired by their favorite characters, and even create stories and artwork that allow them to enter imaginative worlds of their own making. "Anime fandom is a multifaceted world," says Giacco Danielle, a writer for the online magazine Medium. "It's not just about watching anime. It's also about creating, sharing, and celebrating this art form."[1]

Something for Everyone

One of the reasons that anime and manga have such a large fan base is that they appeal to a wide range of demographics, tastes, and interests. When manga first emerged after World War II, the comic narratives were generally divided along gender lines, corresponding to Japanese culture at the time. Comics aimed at boys were known as *shōnen*, and the ones designed for girls were called *shōjo*. Shōnen typically featured male protagonists with storylines of action, adventure, sports, and science fiction. Shōjo featured female main characters in stories of romance or drama. Eventually, the term *kodomomuke* emerged as a description for manga created for children of both genders under age twelve. The terms *shōnen* and *shōjo* were reserved for works appealing to teens.

> **"Anime fandom is a multifaceted world. It's not just about watching anime. It's also about creating, sharing, and celebrating this art form."[1]**
>
> **—Giacco Danielle, writer for Medium**

As postwar shōnen and shōjo readers grew up, so did manga and anime. The term *seinen* was coined to describe works targeted at male readers who are eighteen and older. Seinen stories deal with mature themes, including graphic violence, psychology, and sex. *Josei* is the female counterpart to seinen. Its stories also have no restrictions. They include the same mature themes as seinen does but spend more time exploring relationships.

In the early years of anime and manga, the art forms portrayed traditional gender roles. Today anime and manga are fully LGBTQ+ friendly. They include popular series in two gender-bending categories: *yaoi*, depicting male-to-male relationships, and *yuri*, featuring female-to-female relationships. "Anime and manga can be set in a different time line, where being Queer/ being your self . . . is a social norm," says fan Hacker-chan. "Look at *Witch from Mercury*. *Love Stage*. *Blue Period*. *Ranma 1/2*. The character development is like: 'okay, they are queer . . . sooooo what?'"[2]

Beyond their demographic categories, manga and anime also feature various thematic genres. Among the most popular

Anime and manga fans are a diverse and loyal community. They connect online, meet face-to-face, and even dress up in costumes inspired by their favorite characters.

are *mecha*, stories featuring giant robots; *ecchi*, adult comedies; slice of life, focused on everyday challenges and dramas; and idol, centered on the lives of young, aspiring entertainers. Some categories are devoted to mystical themes. These include *mahou shoujo*, featuring female protagonists with magical powers, and *isekai*, involving main characters who die but are reincarnated in another world.

Inspired by Japanese folklore and Shinto and Buddhist religions, many anime and manga artists depict clashes between figures from different spiritual realms. For example, the main character in Tite Kubo's popular manga series *Bleach* is an ordinary high school student except for the fact that he can see ghosts and is drawn into conflicts with evil spirits. In Shigeru Mizuki's manga and anime series *GeGeGe no Kitarō*, the protagonist is a supernatural being from Japanese folklore who strives to achieve harmony between human beings and supernatural beings.

An Uplifting Escape

Many anime fans find the exploits of their favorite characters uplifting and empowering. "These characters who are brimming with positivity and confidence in themselves often appeal mostly to teens and adults who are shy, withdrawn, and lack confidence," observes Rachael Lefler, a writer for HubPages. "For such people, anime protagonists serve as heroes and role models. Someone they wish they could be like."[3]

"Anime protagonists serve as heroes and role models."[3]

—Rachael Lefler, writer for HubPages

With so much variety—from the silly to the sublime—anime and manga not only appeal to a diverse audience but remain relevant to fans as they grow in age, sophistication, and interests. Some fans even build their education around their love of these popular art forms, hoping to forge a career as an artist, voice actor, cinematographer, sound engineer, or any of the dozens of jobs related to anime and manga production. One thing that all fans of anime and manga share is a chance to temporarily escape the problems of the workaday world and root for their favorite characters as they confront the challenges before them.

CHAPTER ONE

Sharing a Passion

Reading a book or watching a film can be a solo pursuit, and many people are perfectly content to enjoy such works by themselves. But discussing a book or movie with friends often helps a reader or viewer appreciate a work more deeply. Just putting their thoughts into words can help people better understand what they like about a book or film—what moves them, touches them, and makes them feel different or better for having experienced the work of art. Hearing what others have to say about a book or movie can open up new vistas of understanding and appreciation about the work and what it means to others. Like other consumers of films and books, many fans of anime and manga enjoy discussing their favorite works. According to a 2022 survey by the Japanese public relations company Dentsu, 47.7 percent of American manga and anime fans aged eighteen to twenty-four regularly talk about anime and manga with at least one other person.

Online Discussion Groups

Many anime and manga fans share their knowledge, enthusiasm, and passion for these art forms online. Some post their thoughts about a favorite book, movie, or TV series on traditional social media platforms, including TikTok, Instagram, Facebook, and Quora. Others visit platforms dedicated to anime and manga, including Anime Tube, Crunchyroll, MyAnimeList, and Reddit.

Sometimes referred to as "the front page of the internet," Reddit features more than two hundred communities, called subreddits, dedicated to anime and manga. Reddit is a great place to go to find out the latest news in the worlds of anime and manga. Fans express their opinions, post memes, and even share their fan art. The website's system of upvotes and downvotes means that the hottest topics and observations rise to the top, making it easy to find the new and noteworthy. Most posts have links to related topics. Once fans have discovered a topic of interest, they can follow the additional links to a wealth of relevant posts.

MyAnimeList has some overlap with Reddit but caters to fans who enjoy in-depth discussions of anime. The website includes helpful features for dedicated fans. Users can create profiles, log their watch history, and build custom lists of anime films and shows. They can comment on and rank reviews, post their own reviews, and take part in discussions in the forums. MyAnimeList aggregates the user rankings to prioritize its offerings, making it easy to find the highest-quality contributions.

One of the advantages of online fan groups is that they are informal. Fans can participate from home and on their own schedule. Online chats can also be anonymous, with fans being known only

MyAnimeList caters to fans who enjoy in-depth discussions of anime. The website includes helpful features for dedicated fans, and users can create profiles and log their watch history.

> **"Online anime communities create safe havens where fans can engage in in-depth debates and discussions without fear of judgment."[4]**
>
> **—Christian Markle, writer for CBR**

by their usernames. This anonymity can make fans feel safe about expressing their thoughts and feelings. "Online anime communities create safe havens where fans can engage in in-depth debates and discussions without fear of judgment," writes Christian Markle, a writer for the entertainment website CBR. "Anonymity within these platforms provides the freedom for individuals to express their opinions and perspectives openly. Fans delve into plot analyses, dissect character development, and explore the underlying themes of their favorite shows without hesitation."[4]

The anonymity allowed by anime and manga fan sites also makes it safe for fans to express not just their opinions but also their emotions. Fans often say things online that they might be embarrassed to say even to their friends. They can share their excitement over spine-tingling episodes, gush over the actions of their favorite characters, and openly express their loss, regret, and sadness when plotlines take a heartbreaking turn. The ability to express their feelings online and be heard and even comforted by other fans can help anime and manga fans feel less isolated. Even when they do not express their own emotions, seeing posts by others who share their feelings can make fans feel good about themselves. "This emotional outlet creates a strong sense of camaraderie and empathy among fans, as they bond over shared experiences and emotions within the anime world,"[5] says Markle.

Most fans go online to share their enthusiasm for their favorite works, but constructive criticism is also welcome in most fan forums. Some manga and anime fans want the genres to be even more progressive than they are, and they might go online to demand more from the artists and creators. The portrayal of women is of concern to some fans, especially when male storytellers overlook opportunities to give voice and depth to female characters. For example, Melissa Ojeda, a fan of the popular series *My Hero Academia*, written and illustrated by Kōhei Horikoshi, believes the artist's presentation of the female characters could be improved. Says Ojeda:

Some of the best parts of *My Hero Academia* are its characters. Each character has their own personality and development. However, some are far less developed than others—especially the girls. Characters like Nejire of the big three have little to no character development compared to their male counterparts. While characters like Uraraka have some backstory, she still doesn't do as much as the boys. For fans who love the girls in this story, it is incredibly frustrating that *My Hero Academia*'s female cast doesn't get the spotlight they deserve.[6]

The Future of Anime and Manga Online Meetings

Anime and manga often are forward looking, with many stories set in the future. Accordingly, emerging technologies such as virtual reality (VR), augmented reality, and the metaverse are a good fit with anime and manga fan culture. These technologies allow fans to interact with their favorite characters and worlds in a medium known as immersive storytelling. A leader in VR technology, Hololive Production, describes the potential of a metaverse it calls Holoearth:

> The project Holoearth envisions a future where VTubers and fans can interact in a virtual space. . . . The following experiences are expected to take place at Holoearth:
>
> virtual meetups: fans can interact directly with VTubers through their avatars
>
> virtual live performances: fans can enjoy live performances in a 3D space with a more immersive experience
>
> virtual goods: enables fans to collect and trade digital items
>
> fan interaction: a place to interact with fans from around the world in real time.
>
> With the development of VR technology, the ways to enjoy hololive performances will further expand. In the future, wearing a VR headset may make it possible to experience as if you are in the same space as a VTuber.

Neokyo, "A Complete Guide to Enjoying Hololive: Find Your Oshi," August 16, 2024. https://neokyo.com.

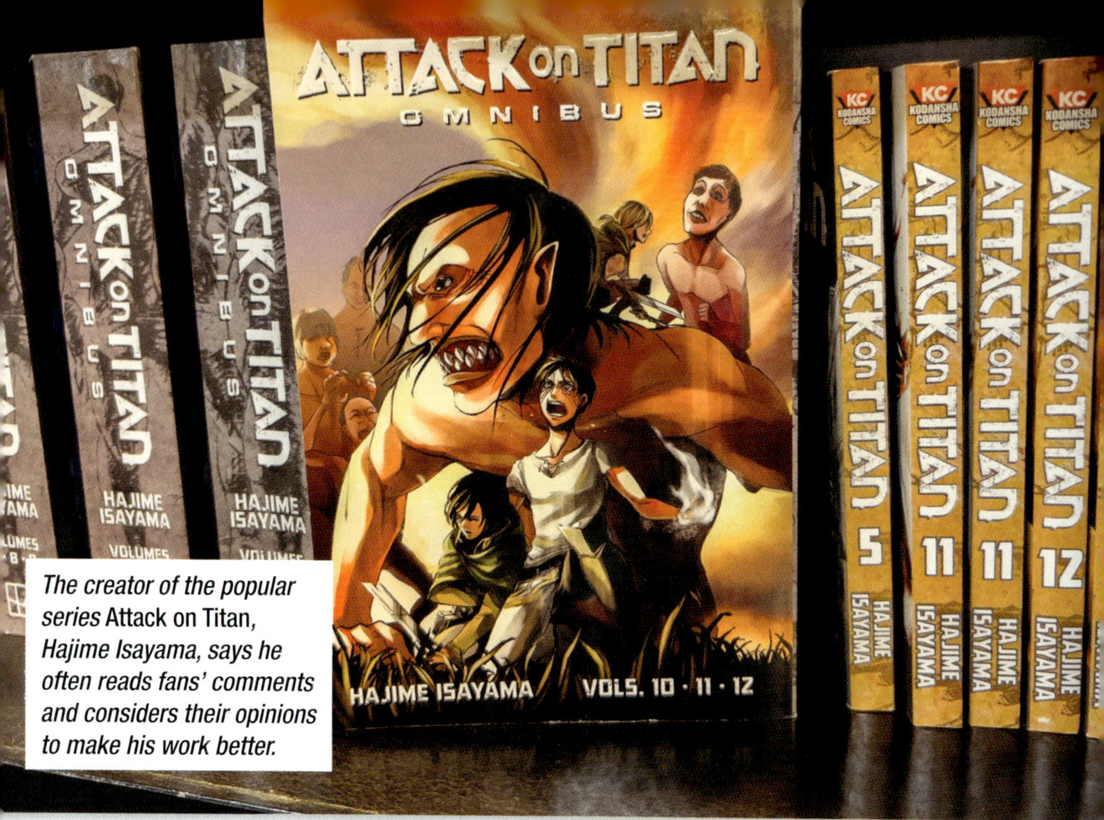

The creator of the popular series Attack on Titan, *Hajime Isayama, says he often reads fans' comments and considers their opinions to make his work better.*

Being able to voice criticism and concerns about anime and manga deepens the bond that fans have with the art forms. Having offered their opinion, critical fans will often watch to see if future episodes confirm it. They may also hope that the changes they call for are adopted by the author. It is not inconceivable that the artist would respond to such criticism. Hajime Isayama, the creator of the popular series *Attack on Titan*, told the mangabrog blog that he often reads fans' comments and considers their opinions to make his work better.

Virtual Fan Clubs

With the advances in online video technology, anime and manga fans also connect with each other using videoconferencing apps like Zoom, Google Hangouts, or Jitsi. In addition, there are dozens of anime and manga communities that hold video chats on platforms like Discord, WhatsApp, and Telegram. The online service Meetup enables people to create groups that host local in-person and virtual events.

Virtual gatherings allow members to discuss their favorite series, share theories about plotlines, and celebrate their favorite characters together without having to type or dictate words on a screen. They also offer a wider range of activities than text-based forums can. Members of virtual groups can share their screens with others logged on to the session to play video clips of their favorite characters or series. Online groups can hold watch parties of new anime episodes as they are released. And fans can show off merchandise they have purchased or costumes they have made. These live meetings help decrease participants' isolation. Because some people attend their virtual events regularly over long periods, they can get to know each other well and even form friendships. "In my personal experience, I have made many friends who have become like my family in fandom spaces," says writer A.J. Riley. "I met my best friends through our love of shows, music, books, movies, etc. Fandoms can be very special to many people."[7]

In-Person Clubs and Gatherings

Some anime and manga fans never feel a need to venture beyond their online activities. Others, however, are interested in face-to-face contact. Such fans may start or join school clubs devoted to anime, manga, or both. These clubs exist at many levels—middle school, high school, and college. School clubs provide even more options for bonding with other devotees of the Japanese art forms and Japanese culture than online communities do. They also break down the social stigma that lingers around anime and manga fandom. Says Alden Parker, a member of the Amherst College anime club:

> Before, simply having an interest in this stuff could more easily have gotten you side looks from behind the scenes, or comments such as "oh, you're one of those people." This is why I got most of my initial exposure through reading, as

even bringing anime up with friends could have been too much of a risk. Whereas now, I can be very open about my interests in anime especially because of the anime club. So the increase in popularity has been overwhelmingly positive in my opinion.[8]

Like online groups, school clubs have watch parties, hold in-depth discussions about books and films, and sponsor costume shows. But they can also do things that are difficult or impossible to do online. For example, some hold all-night watch-a-thons, have board game tournaments, and even go on field trips. They might attend an anime movie premiere or go to nearby anime and manga conventions. For many young people, it is often easier to go to events with a group than to go by themselves. Being part of a club makes the world of anime and manga more accessible to them. "Anime Club provides a centralized anime-viewing experience," writes Fritz Lalley, a student at Amherst College in Amherst, Massachusetts. "There are no strings attached. There is no commitment. There is no entrance fee. No pressure. Beyond simply watching anime, the club provides a setting for robust discussion and debate regarding the themes and messages of relevant shows."[9]

"Before, simply having an interest in this stuff could more easily have gotten you side looks from behind the scenes, or comments such as 'oh, you're one of those people.' . . . Now, I can be very open about my interests in anime especially because of the anime club."[8]

—Alden Parker, member of the Amherst College anime club

Many anime and manga clubs not only explore their favorite art forms but also delve into Japanese culture. They may go to an anime-themed café or to a traditional Japanese restaurant. They might attend a Japanese exhibit at a museum, a Japanese theatrical production, or a Japanese musical event. An anime and manga fan who has an intense interest in the comics and Japanese culture in general is often referred to as an *otaku*. "Ideally, the modern anime club is a cultural exchange committee, where a group of fans, steeped in anime and *otaku*

Anime and Manga Clubs for Minority Communities

Some anime and manga fan clubs cater to specific demographic groups. For example, Black Anime Nerds, with 37,400 members, and Black Anime Society, with 31,600 members, are private Facebook groups appealing to Black Americans. Anime Latino, appealing to Spanish-speaking fans, and Filipino Anime Lovers Club, appealing to Tagalog- and English-speaking fans with roots in the Philippines, are popular groups on MyAnimeList.

LGBTQ Anime Fans and LGBTQ+ Anime Austin are clubs founded especially for lesbian, gay, bisexual, transgender, and queer or questioning anime fans. These clubs are meant to provide an extra level of comfort and camaraderie for members of minority communities. "I've been a member of LGBTQ+ Anime Austin since 2020, when I was early in transition," says Holly. "I've always been an introvert, but they've done so much to help me feel less alone. When I show up to a meetup, they're always happy to see me."

Holly, email interview with the author, November 18, 2024.

culture, share context and perspective with one another, and share context and perspective with the community,"[10] says Iyashikei, a writer for Medium.

In addition to schools, other individuals and groups have established independent anime and manga fan clubs. These fan clubs cater mainly to teens and young adults. They allow fans to continue their involvement with other fans even after leaving school. The online service Meetup allows people to create groups that host local in-person and virtual events. It has 570 groups in 299 cities worldwide that are devoted to anime and manga. Some Meetup groups are interested in all types of anime and manga, while others specialize in certain genres. Some groups meet in person; others connect online.

Mega Events

Conventions and expositions are the grandest and most sophisticated gatherings of anime and manga fans. Nearly every major US city has an anime or manga expo. Anime Expo, held in Los

Angeles, is the largest anime convention in North America. The 2024 event drew more than 392,000 attendees from 60 countries and featured more than 400 exhibitors, showcasing the latest in anime, manga, video games, and entertainment. Attendees spent an estimated $95 million over the four-day event. Other large anime and manga conventions in the United States include Comic-Con in San Diego, Youmacon in Detroit, and Otakon in Washington, DC.

It is not uncommon for movie studios and manga publishers to announce their new releases, show trailers of upcoming movies, or even hold world premieres of new anime films at major

Conventions and expositions are the grandest and most sophisticated gatherings of anime and manga fans. Nearly every major US city has an anime or manga expo.

conventions. For example, the anime film *Sand Land*, based on the manga by Akira Toriyama, the creator of the world's most popular manga series, *Dragon Ball*, received its world premiere at the 2023 Comic-Con. "Anime conventions serve as a melting pot where all these passions come together, creating a vibrant and diverse tapestry of fandom,"[11] observes Giacco Danielle.

Organizers of the expos invite top anime and manga creators, directors, voice actors, and producers to serve as guest speakers or panel members. The 2024 Anime Expo in Los Angeles hosted the cast members of the motion picture *My Hero Academia: You're Next*, including voice actors Mamoru Miyano (Giulio), Daiki Yamashita (Izuku), Kenta Miyake (All Might), and Meru Nukumi (Anna). It also celebrated the fifth anniversary of the anime series *Demon Slayer: Kimetsu no Yaiba* with voice actors Natsuki Hanae (Tanjiro) and Takahiro Sakurai (Giyu) and producer Yūma Takahashi.

Meeting the Stars

Fans not only get to see their idols when they speak to large groups, they can get even closer to them at autograph sessions. Not all the stars participate in autograph sessions, but many do. For example, at the 2024 Anime Expo, more than two hundred anime producers, directors, artists, authors, and voice actors signed autographs over the four-day event. Some anime pros charge for their autographs. Others—especially guests of honor—do not. Typically, celebrities will exchange a few words with autograph seekers as they sign fans' programs, artwork, or whatever they want their idols to sign. Some artists even include a sketch with their autograph. For example, Hideaki Anno, creator of the *Evangelion* franchise, and Yusuke Kozaki, manga artist and character artist for anime and games, include drawings with their autographs.

Getting a personalized work from a favorite artist can be thrilling experience for a dedicated fan. Writes Moonbear Tsukino, a blogger on Amino, a social media platform for communities dedicated to shared interests:

> I'm still fangirling over meeting Yusuke Kozaki himself at Anime Expo and getting a Kagero sketch. . . . It was so mesmerizing watching Yusuke draw in person because Kagero came out beautifully. I was this close to crying tears of joy. I can die happy because I achieved my dream of getting a Kagero sketch drawn by the artist who designed her. This has been a very memorable Anime Expo indeed.[12]

The autograph sessions can be rewarding for the anime and manga professionals as well. The storytellers can learn which of their creations are having the biggest impact on their fans and what fans are looking for in the future. "We live in a bubble sometimes, and you can get out of touch with your fans," says Kunal Nayyar, star of *The Big Bang Theory* and voice-over actor for several animated films. "You go to the studio, you come home. But coming to Comic-Con is a real opportunity to connect with the people that made your show happen and are responsible for its continued success. It's really humbling."[13]

With speakers, panels, autograph sessions, movie screenings, interactive workshops, and an exhibit hall crammed with displays and merchandise, anime and manga conventions can be a bit overwhelming for some attendees, especially first-timers. In addition, many attendees dress up in costumes inspired by their favorite anime and manga characters, a practice known as cosplay, a portmanteau made up from the words *costume* and *play*. Dressed in costumes from the outlandish to the sublime, the cosplayers lend a carnival atmosphere to the activities. "Comic-Con is interesting because there's so much going on at once, it's literally impossible to do everything," says comedian and animated film voice actor Chris Hardwick. "You need clones and some sort of hoverboard so you can surf over the crowd."[14]

The bigger the anime and manga conventions get, the more celebrities and premieres they attract. The more stars who attend, the more media coverage the events receive, and the more fans flock to the venues. Tickets for the biggest events sell out in minutes. Attendees sleep outside in line the night before the doors open just to be sure they can get into the sessions they want to attend. Social media influencers live stream from the events. The gaming platform IGN live streams conventions worldwide. "Comic-Con has become more of a pop cultural festival, and to not be included feels like you're missing the biggest celebration of the year,"[15] says actor, producer, writer, and streamer Felicia Day.

"Comic-Con has become more of a pop cultural festival, and to not be included feels like you're missing the biggest celebration of the year."[15]

—Felicia Day, actor, producer, writer, and streamer

All the buzz around the anime and manga events also arouses the curiosity of outsiders, leading many to sample the Japanese art forms for the first time and making fans of some of them. The circle of fandom expands. Anime and manga sales increase, attendance at clubs and expos swells, and the cycle of growth continues. "The future of anime and manga is bright, with both industries continuing to grow and expand globally," writes Trey Bates, an educator and freelance writer. "Overall, the future of anime and manga is dynamic and exciting, with endless possibilities for creativity and innovation."[16]

CHAPTER TWO

The World of Cosplay

On August 3, 2024, two actors crouched on the darkened stage of the Aichi Arts Center Main Hall in Nagoya, Japan. From offstage the audience heard the name of the popular anime and manga series *Naruto*. And with that the presentation began. The screen behind the stage lit up with a scene from *Naruto*—a black-and-white image of a waterfall. When the stage lights came up, the actors, clad in costumes depicting the ninja warriors Naruto Uzumaki and Sasuke Uchiha, the main characters of *Naruto*, began to move around each other in a carefully choreographed fight sequence of jumps, kicks, and cartwheels. As the screen behind them morphed into images of flames and then stone, the characters upped the intensity of their battle into fire ball jutsu and then into shadow clone jutsu, two of the mystical battle arts.

Suddenly, the stage went dark. When the lights came up again a moment later, the actors were twirling around under giant cloth clouds of orange and blue, the colors associated with each of the warriors. As the crowd cheered, the swirling fabric inflated from within, forming giant balloons depicting the characters' avatars, Kurama and Susanoo. The outsized beings clashed in a dance-like battle. The lights went out again, but this time the stage was not completely dark. The avatars, illuminated from within, continued to fight. The crowd, now on its feet, roared its approval. At last, Kurama struck a decisive blow, and the screen behind the stage flashed with a simulated explosion. The avatar balloons collapsed on the stage, and the warriors met in the middle of the stage. Sasuke presented Naruto with a cape as a sign of his respect for his rival's victory.

An Award-Winning Performance

For such a stunning and extravagant performance, the actors, Mamemayo and Mioshi, were crowned champions at the 2024 World Cosplay Summit, a celebration of cosplay and culture held in Nagoya, Japan, since 2003. They received gold medals and $30,000 in prize money for their presentation. "We're grateful to our teachers who taught us how to make the costumes and hone our performance," said Mamemayo in Japanese. "Most of all, it's thanks to those of you here today who supported us and perfected our performance. Thanks a lot, *dattebayo*,"[17] Mamemayo added, signing off with Naruto Uzumaki's catchphrase meaning, "believe it."

The World Cosplay Summit is the largest cosplay organization in the world. In 2024 cosplay teams from thirty-nine countries

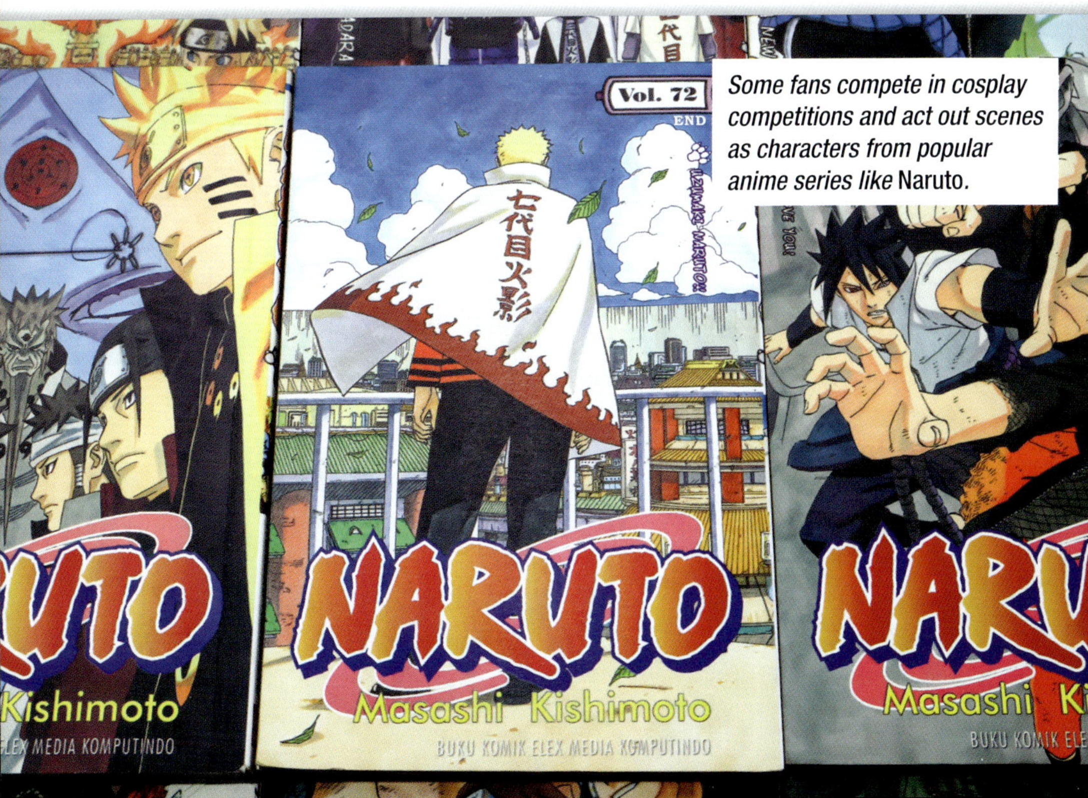

Some fans compete in cosplay competitions and act out scenes as characters from popular anime series like Naruto.

competed for the grand championship in Nagoya. The two-person teams can portray characters from Japanese anime, manga, video games, or *tokusatsu* (live-action films or television programs that make heavy use of practical special effects). Characters from live-action movies or stage productions based on anime or manga are not permitted. The costumes must be homemade, not purchased. Friends can work on the costumes, but the participants must do much of the work. There are size and weight limits for the costumes.

Considering that manga and anime are Japanese art forms, it might not be surprising that Mamemayo and Mioshi, representing Japan, won the 2024 World Cosplay Summit grand prize. However, it was the first time in twelve years that a Japanese team had prevailed. At the 2024 summit, the Swedish team placed second. The cosplayers depicted the young girl Satsuki and the giant, cuddly spirit Totoro from Hayao Miyazaki's anime *My Neighbor Totoro*. Team Germany came in third with their presentation of the Nintendo role-playing game *Monster Hunter XX*. Additional prizes were given in the categories of Best Costume, Best Armor, Most Emotional Performance, and Most Excellent Action. The World Cosplay Summit also sponsors a cinematic cosplay competition, which is broadcast live on Facebook, Twitch, X (formerly Twitter), and YouTube. The cinematic grand prize went to the team from Latvia, with Mexico finishing second and China coming in third. The organization also sponsors the Gamers8 Cosplay Cup in Riyadh, Saudi Arabia, which features more than one hundred cosplay teams from forty-five countries vying for the $100,000 Cosplay Cup grand prize.

A Popular Hobby

Each country participating in the World Cosplay Summit holds preliminary competitions, attracting thousands of participants worldwide. The World Cosplay Summit USA Finals are held at the Anime Expo in Los Angeles. The finals are preceded by regional preliminary competitions across the country. Cosplay hobbyists

Building Human Connections Through Cosplay

An experienced cosplayer, Brandon Kelly believes that cosplay can be a source of personal growth and a means to empathize with others. He writes:

> Placing yourself in someone else's shoes (real or fictional) can teach morals and wisdom. . . .
>
> As a result of seeing parts of myself in a fictional character, it's easier to see the oneness of real people around me. In the same way I can see myself as a character, I find out that I am also the person standing next to me on the subway. I am also the person sitting down, waiting at the door, and the one reading a book. I empathize and sympathize with them more because I believe I am them. I see reality through their eyes, and I am less judgmental because of it. . . .
>
> Cosplay brings you closer to strangers. It can teach someone to look for similarities between people rather than divide them by differences. . . .
>
> You're not doing this to gain attention. It's not about you, but the people's lives you touch. You are doing this to spread love. . . . Cosplay is not only good for fun, but it builds connections between people that may otherwise never have existed.

Brandon Kelly, "Fun Ways Cosplay Can Win You a Golden Ticket to Heaven," Medium, October 2, 2024. https://medium.com.

from all walks of life participate not only in the World Cosplay Summit events but also in local cosplay competitions held year-round in the United States.

Most cosplayers are not into it for the money or competition. They do it for fun and to bond with other fans. A study conducted by researchers at East Texas A&M University finds that 30 percent of anime fans self-identify as coplayers. "Cosplay has become a popular hobby around the world and has grown into a large and diverse community," states the *Anime Costume Blog*. "Whether it's for personal enjoyment or for competitions and events, cosplay is a fun and creative way for fans to bring their favorite characters to life."[18]

One of the most popular activities for cosplayers is to connect with other fans by posting photographs of themselves in their costumes online. Instagram alone has more than 68 million posts with the hashtag cosplay. The anime website Crunchyroll features more than 1,000 pages of cosplay photos from amateurs and professionals alike. Most cosplayers take their own photos, but some attend photo shoot events to have their pictures taken by a professional. Some of these professionals charge for their services, but many photo events are free, especially at conventions or around holidays like Halloween and Christmas. Dedicated cosplayers look for upcoming photo events on social media sites and plan accordingly.

Some cosplayers have used Instagram and TikTok to launch their careers as social media influencers. Model, cosplayer, and social media influencer Princess Sachiko has an astounding 19.2 million followers on TikTok, 3.4 million followers on YouTube, and 1 million followers on Instagram. Her TikTok videos have received more than 346 million likes. The media analyst firm Social Blade estimates that Princess Sachiko's YouTube earnings alone total up to $430,000 a year.

A Personal Journey

For many fans of anime and manga, cosplay is not just a social activity. It is a journey of self-discovery and self-expression that they experience as they immerse themselves in the planning, making, and wearing of costumes. Not only do fans create costumes inspired by characters, they often mimic the way the characters move and speak their catchphrases. Fans use the costume to become the characters they admire, giving them the opportunity to act in ways that might be liberating from their everyday selves. "Every time I put on a cosplay costume, I immediately feel like I'm transformed into a new person," says a cosplayer named Joyce. "It's kind of an experience of changing my identity."[19]

> "Every time I put on a cosplay costume, I immediately feel like I'm transformed into a new person. It's kind of an experience of changing my identity."[19]
>
> —Joyce, cosplayer

The temporary transformation that cosplayers experience can make them feel better about themselves. "Cosplay can be particularly empowering," explains psychologist Drea Letamendi. "It allows someone to experience and explore the feelings of being in control, actualizing freedom, being heroic, or sensing oneself as physically strong, revered and respected."[20] Morgan Looney, a special effects makeup artist and cosmetology student, says she has gained confidence through cosplay. "The main reason why I love cosplay so much is because it provides some sort of escape from reality," she says. "As someone who hasn't been the strongest

For many fans of anime and manga, cosplay is not just a social activity. It is a journey of self-expression as they immerse themselves in the planning, making, and wearing of costumes.

“As someone who hasn’t been the strongest person and has often felt alone in the world, cosplay and going to conventions brought me into a whole new atmosphere of supportive and accepting people that I didn’t know existed.”[21]

—Morgan Looney, cosplayer

person and has often felt alone in the world, cosplay and going to conventions brought me into a whole new atmosphere of supportive and accepting people that I didn’t know existed.”[21]

For Ace, a cosplayer in California, dressing in a costume and taking on the attributes of a character do not disguise her personality. They reveal it. Cosplay takes the focus off her everyday physical appearance and lets her inner self shine through. “It’s a part of my personal growth, part of the way I connect with the rest of the world,” she says. “I think cosplay is a window for the world to see a part of me that’s outside of my appearance.”[22]

Connecting with a Character

The cosplay experience begins with selecting a character that resonates personally or presents a creative challenge. The fan then researches costume details, gathering and studying character images and noting the details in the character’s clothing, hair, expressions, and movements. Is the character associated with certain items that can be staged as props? But the research is not always concerned with outward things. The character’s background, personality, and conflicts are also considered.

When the cosplayer plans to compete, reproducing the character’s appearance down to the smallest detail is important. For example, the award-winning cosplayer Mamemayo not only recreated Naruto Uzumaki’s spikey yellow hair, black headband with a silver medallion, black shirt, and orange trousers, she took the time to smudge the clothing with dirt and soot and even fray the fabric by hand so her costume matched Naruto’s battered appearance at the end of his climactic battle with Sasuke Uchiha. Judges in high-stakes cosplay competitions expect the entrants to create highly accurate versions of the characters they are portraying, and fidelity to the original drawings is highly rewarded.

But not all competitions are looking for perfect copies of the characters' appearance. Some, especially at the fan club level, make room for individual interpretation of the characters. In addition, many cosplayers are less interested in competition than self-expression, and they enjoy taking liberties with the characters. "Depending on how I want the costume to look, depends on how accurate it will be to the character," a cosplayer told Ashley Lotecki, a researcher at Toronto Metropolitan University. "I've taken a Kingdom Hearts Cosplay of Kairi and completely transformed it into what I thought she'd look like if she ever visited Halloween

Cosplay and Confidence

A self-described nerdy writer who loves anime, Giacco Danielle describes cosplay as a journey of self-discovery.

> Cosplay is a celebration, a carnival of individuality. It's about saying, Hey, this is me, and I love it! Whether you're a bookworm, a gamer, or a superhero enthusiast, there's a character out there waiting for you to embody them and let your uniqueness shine. Crafting a cosplay is not just about creating a costume; it's an expedition into the realms of self-discovery. As you choose, design, and wear your cosplay, you might surprise yourself with what you uncover. It's like peeling back layers to reveal the awesome person beneath the everyday facade.
>
> Cosplay is a safe space to step out of your comfort zone. Embodying a character allows you to explore facets of yourself that you might not often reveal. It's a confidence booster, a way to break free from everyday constraints and embrace the boundless possibilities of who you can be. In the world of cosplay, you're never alone. It's a global community where individuals from all walks of life come together to share their passion. Whether you're a beginner or a seasoned cosplayer, there's always someone cheering you on, ready to celebrate the uniqueness you bring to the cosplay stage.

Giacco Danielle, "The Art of Cosplay: Crafting Your Identity at Anime Conventions," Medium, November 20, 2023. https://medium.com.

Town. Not only did I envision the outfit, I also envisioned the keyblade that she'd have with it."[23]

Some cosplayers take their reimagining of a character even further, creating a backstory that reveals the character's personality. "If I'm not cosplaying as a character from a pre-existing story, I like to write the background of my character, maybe write a short story about them, and imagine him in different circumstances," says one cosplayer. "I think about what my character does for work, what's his rank in society, and try to design the costume from that."[24]

A Practical Endeavor

Experienced cosplayers advise that after settling on the look of the character, designers should create a budget for the costume. This includes estimating costs not only of the materials that will be used in the costume—such as fabrics, thermoplastics, foam, and wigs—but also of the tools that will be necessary to craft the materials. If cosplayers are thinking of entering a competition, the

Making a costume can be daunting for first-time cosplayers. Experienced cosplayers advise that after settling on the look of the character, designers should create a budget for the costume.

costs of entry fees, transportation, and in some cases even lodging must be factored in.

Starting a costume can be daunting, especially for first-time cosplayers. Fortunately, there are many resources available online. The website Cosplay Advice has step-by-step instructions on how to make all kinds of costumes and accessories—from hair bows to boot covers, and everything in between. Many of the items—especially shoe and book covers, body armor, and even talons with movable joints—are made with ethylene-vinyl acetate (EVA) foam, a lightweight foam material known for its flexibility. The light weight is important, especially if the costume includes extremely elaborate features such as armor, weapons, and wings. A costume that is heavy can be difficult to wear. In addition, many cosplay competitions have weight limitations. For example, all equipment, costumes, and props for the World Cosplay Summit USA Finals performance are limited to a maximum weight of 88.18 pounds (40 kg) combined for both performers.

EVA foam can be heated and molded into a shape that the material will hold when it cools. Cosplayers can apply texture to EVA foam and paint it for realistic effects, making facsimiles of everything from leather to metal. Other items, such as eye masks and full-face masks, are made with cardboard and papier-mâché. Cosplay Advice lists materials needed for each type of mask and shows patterns for cutting the foam, cardboard, and cloth. Many of the pages include videos that guide the cosplayer through the process. The website also has ideas for jewelry and makeup—even how to make freckles.

When it comes to making costumes, cosplayers need to decide whether their priority is accuracy or comfort. If planning to compete, cosplayers will likely try to make their costumes as accurate as possible. Even some noncompetitive cosplayers believe the whole point is to make a costume as close to the original as possible and that it is worth a little discomfort to achieve their goal. "I for one will always forego comfort for accuracy," says cosplayer Starlit Rose. "I really don't care about my comfort level

> "I for one will always forego comfort for accuracy. I really don't care about my comfort level when I cosplay. I have too much fun wearing the costumes to notice most of the time anyway."[25]
>
> —Starlit Rose, cosplayer

when I cosplay . . . I have too much fun wearing the costumes to notice most of the time anyway."[25]

Others, though, are willing to compromise, especially if they plan to spend the whole day in costume at a convention or expo. "If there isn't a huge discrepancy between the original and your cosplay, I would go for comfort," says a cosplayer who goes by the pseudonym SweeneyTodd. "For example, my shoes I use for my cosplay have been really hurting me. And although they make me taller and look better with my costume, I will never wear them again at a convention."[26] The whole point of cosplay, says cosplayer Knockabout, is to have fun and not worry too much about faithfulness to the original:

> People change cosplays all the time, whether it's for comfort, religious purposes, practicality, or extra style. You're good—do whatever makes you most comfortable. No one will think anything of it. Cosplay's really about just trying to show the "spirit" of the character; most people are not going for a 1-to-1 accurate reproduction, especially since it can be actively impossible a lot of the time.[27]

Choosing How to Cosplay

For many dedicated cosplayers, however, there are limits to how much license to take with the original design. They believe that cosplayers should remain faithful to the artist's' creations. "It's not difficult to tell who is a real cosplayer and who is not," a cosplayer named Chelsea told researchers at Toronto Metropolitan University. "The most obvious indicator is that their costumes do not match the original character in terms of style and color. I saw a cosplayer even wearing sneakers with an ancient outfit."[28] In the same survey, a cosplayer named Ivy added, "Some people are superficial and insincere. They like to cosplay because they think this is a trend. I don't think they really understand what cosplay is."[29] The researchers noted, "In other words, authentic cosplayers should display interest, affection, and involvement. This opinion was shared by several other cosplayers."[30]

Whether done for fun or profit, as a one-time lark or a long-term pastime, cosplay can be an entertaining and even enlightening experience. For some, like eighteen-year-old cosplayer Moon, cosplay promotes personal growth. "Cosplay is a method of expression and escapism and a way to be someone else, even just for a few hours," he says. "With cosplay, I feel more confident and comfortable in myself, and it makes me feel like I'm able to do things I'm normally not able to do. It also helps me express myself in ways that I normally struggle to express."[31]

CHAPTER THREE

Artistic Endeavors

Many fans of anime and manga are content to experience the adventures of their heroes vicariously, watching them in action or reading about their exploits. Other fans yearn for a deeper connection. Some engage in cosplay, dressing like their favorite characters and even portraying them at anime and manga events. Others enter the imaginary realms of anime and manga by writing stories or drawing scenes based on existing works. Written works of this type are known as fan fiction. Illustrated works are known as fan art. "When you find something you really like, it's sometimes hard to express how much it's influencing your life," explains KK Miller, an American writer living in Japan. "To show off how much they love something, some fans try cosplay or rampant consumerism. Others write songs or fan fiction to tell the world the extent of their affection. But for others, it's as simple as drawing a picture that perfectly captures all their feelings on the paper."[32]

> **"To show off how much they love something, some fans try cosplay or rampant consumerism. Others write songs or fan fiction to tell the world the extent of their affection. But for others, it's as simple as drawing a picture that perfectly captures all their feelings on the paper."[32]**
>
> —KK Miller, writer

Fan fiction and fan art allow for the exploration of themes and storylines not covered in the original works. The fans may place well-known characters in novel situations, give them new goals, and even reveal their thoughts through speech and action. In some cases experimenting with fan fiction and fan art inspires writers and artists to create their own original anime and manga characters and stories.

Fan fiction and fan art are an important part of anime and manga fan culture. These pursuits deepen the connection amateur writers and artists have with the anime and manga characters and series that inspire them. This bond keeps fan fiction writers and fan artists interested in the series they are following, priming them to attend new anime films or purchase new manga releases. The activity also draws new people into the world of anime and manga fandom.

Inspired by Characters

Anime and manga fans who create fan fiction and fan art do so for many reasons, but Rachael Lefler, a writer for HubPages, believes most fans are moved to create their own works because of the characters they admire and what those characters represent to them. "Most anime fans become interested in their favorite shows because they like the characters," writes Lefler. "They want to draw them, act like them, dress up as them, and so on."[33] The amateur writers and artists often feel close enough to

Anime and manga fans who create fan fiction and art do so for many reasons. Most fans create their own works because of the characters they admire and what those characters represent to them.

their characters to sense what the characters might say and do in certain situations. They let their imaginations create new and challenging situations and then let their knowledge of the character take over, using their trademark knowledge, powers, and phrases.

The experience can be empowering for the fan fiction or fan art creators, because they can experience what it is like to be the character as they face new challenges of the creator's making. Lefler observes:

> Their favorite characters are usually young, aesthetically pleasing, and possess desirable traits like confidence, determination, and a positive attitude. Usually in anime, since it's often aimed at teens, a youthful hero or team of heroes has to save the day from corrupt evil people who are older, wiser, and more experienced, but who often have a sad, bitter, jaded outlook in life. So anime resonates well with people who value positive thinking and a can-do attitude, especially when thinking about the popular teen-focused categories of [shōnen] and [shōjo].[34]

Popular Platforms

The enthusiasm of amateur writers and artists can be contagious because many of them share their work on social media platforms that millions of people regularly visit. The most popular fan fiction platform is Wattpad. It has more than 94 million monthly users who spend more than 23 billion minutes a month reading the1 billion original stories uploaded to the platform. In 2021 Wattpad merged with WEBTOON, the world's largest digital comics platform, creating a combined audience of 166 million people. The anime and manga fan fiction and fan art posted on the site build loyalty toward the popular series that the works are based on.

The most popular fan fiction platform is Wattpad. It has more than 94 million monthly users who spend more than 23 billion minutes a month reading the 1 billion original stories on the platform.

Wattpad is not the only popular fan fiction and fan art platform. The website FanFiction has more than 12 million registered users and more than 2 million anime and manga fan fiction stories. Another popular fan fiction website is Archive of Our Own (AO3), a nonprofit, fan-created platform. AO3 allows users to make profiles, publish works, create collections, participate in challenges, and import works. AO3 not only enables the posting of fan fiction and fan art, it also provides a forum for fan videos and podfic (fan fiction read aloud as in a podcast). As of 2023, AO3 had 6 million registered users from around the world and hosted more than 11 million fan works.

In addition to giving fan fiction writers, fan artists, videographers, and podcasters access to a global audience, the fan fiction and fan art platforms are also a source of valuable feedback. All the platforms provide a way for users to comment on the published works. Sometimes the criticism can be harsh, but University of Washington researchers Katie Davis and Cecilia Aragon have found that most of the feedback that fan fiction authors receive is positive. Davis and Aragon analyzed forty-five hundred reviews chosen at random from among the millions of reviews posted on FanFiction. They found that only 1 percent of the reviews they analyzed were nonconstructive negative reviews.

Inspired to Write

Most fan fiction and fan art creators find reader feedback—positive and negative—to be helpful. In 2024 researchers Cecilia Aragon and Sourojit Ghosh surveyed 369 fan fiction writers about their experiences publishing online. They found that most fan fiction writers value the feedback they receive. One fan fiction author told the researchers, "There was this one person who wrote really detailed reviews, going almost paragraph by paragraph for each chapter. I really liked how they did it and so when I wrote my first review, I tried to do it like that. I figured it would be really helpful to the author."[35]

Aragon and Ghosh find that many readers of fan fiction are inspired to try writing it themselves. One survey respondent told Aragon and Ghosh, "I'd found another writer in my fandom at the time who had written dozens of stories that appealed to some of my niche interests, and he wrote a lot about his process of writing and ideation and character sketches and getting over writer's block. In many ways, he's what convinced me to try writing."[36] Another respondent told Aragon and Ghosh that she was inspired to write when she found that one of her favorite fan fiction authors was not raised in an English-speaking home: "English isn't my first language so, in spite of having many ideas, I wasn't confident enough to post something. I was very surprised when I realized one of my favorite writers is Korean, and English is also not her first language, so I thought that if she can do it then I can try too."[37]

There is a great deal of openness and honesty on the fan fiction websites, and hearing about the personal challenges some fan fiction writers face can inspire those who have challenges of their own. "I suffer from a lot of social anxiety, and so I benefited greatly from seeing lots of authors and reviewers acknowledge

A Hidden Form of Mentoring

Researchers Cecilia Aragon and Sourojit Ghosh use the term *lurkers* to identify people who read fan fiction and the comments but do not contribute themselves. Aragon and Ghosh say that lurking is common and not problematic in fan communities. In fact, in the realm of fan fiction, lurkers are often moved to begin writing by observing the positive atmosphere and creativity in online platforms. In this way the active participants become mentors to the lurkers. Aragon and Ghosh maintain that

> such transitions are greatly supported by the formation of incidental mentorship networks amid a supportive community, as lurkers draw motivation from seeing their favorite active users provide behind-the-scenes glimpses into their writing processes and struggles. Such incidental mentorship networks form without the knowledge of active users, at no extra labor on their part, and yet become pivotal to lurkers.

The researchers hope that fan communities will seek new ways to encourage lurkers to engage so that they feel included and are inspired to be active in celebrating their interests.

Sourojit Ghosh and Cecilia Aragon, "Leveraging Community Support and Platform Affordances on a Path to More Active Participation: A Study of Online Fan Fiction Communities," Transformative Works and Cultures, March 14, 2024. https://journal.transformativeworks.org.

their own social anxieties and push through to put themselves out there, and that honestly showed me that even with this anxiety, I can write,"[38] says one fan fiction writer.

The support on display in the comments sections of fan fiction platforms encourages some readers to come out of the shadows and publish their own stories. "Participants [of the survey] who went through periods of readership before becoming active all spoke about the importance of the incredibly positive nature of the community, which alleviated concerns about their work receiving harsh criticism," Aragon and Ghosh write. "While this positivity is not ensured by any particular platform affordances on spaces such as Fanfiction.net and AO3, it has become a noticeable norm and feature of fan communities."[39]

> **"Fan-fic is one big giant writing workshop, one that's voluntarily joined and cranks on and on."[40]**
>
> —N.K. Jemisin, Hugo Award–winning fantasy author

One of those who credits fan fiction with encouraging her to write is fantasy author N.K. Jemisin, the only writer to receive the Hugo Award for best science-fiction or fantasy novel three years in a row. She says that she discovered fan fiction while studying counseling in graduate school. "I was miserable and lonely. I didn't have a lot of friends, or stress relief," Jemisin recalls. "Around then was when I became internetted, and one of the first communities I discovered was a fan-fic community." Intrigued by the stories she read and the online discussions she had with authors and other fans, Jemisin decided to give fan fiction a try. She began writing fan fiction about *Dragon Ball Z* and other favorite series. The activity, she says, "blew the cobwebs off writing abilities I hadn't used since college." The critiques she received from other fans helped her sharpen her storytelling. "Fan-fic is one big giant writing workshop," Jemisin says, "one that's voluntarily joined and cranks on and on."[40]

The Pleasures of Shipping

Part of the fun of fan fiction and fan art is putting characters into new situations and seeing how they navigate the new environment. Fans can put their characters up against new antagonists, send them to a new planet, or somehow change any superpowers they might have. One popular innovation is to pair two or more characters in a romantic relationship, often creating a pairing that does not exist in the original story. This practice is known as shipping. The term arose in 1993, when fans of the television program *The X-Files* created fan fiction portraying a romantic relationship between the program's main characters, Fox Mulder and Dana Scully. These creative fans were dubbed "relationshippers." During the 1990s the term was shortened to "shippers" and was applied to all fan fiction writers and fan artists who paired popular characters who were not together in the original story.

The term "shipping" arose when fans of the television program The X-Files *created fan fiction portraying a romantic relationship between the program's main characters, Fox Mulder (left) and Dana Scully.*

Sometimes fans "ship" characters within the same story because the creator of the series is creating a "slow burn," or a relationship that is developing at an agonizingly slow pace. Fans often want to speed up the process, and they delight in creating the circumstances that can bring the attraction out into the open. "When characters have great chemistry, fans can't help but see the potential for something deeper,"[41] says Effie Sapuridis, a graduate student in media studies at Western University in London, Ontario, Canada.

Shipping is not only fun, it can also contribute to a shipper's well-being, says Sapuridis. That is because shipping allows the fans to experience new and exciting emotions without facing the challenges of a real relationship. Sapuridis explains:

> Fans often become deeply invested in fictional couples because they empathize with and feel connected to the characters. When we can put ourselves in the shoes of the character, we become more invested in their story. Fans connect with characters, and then yearn for their happiness because it feels connected to their own happiness. It becomes more than just a story; instead, shipping the characters becomes a way for fans to explore their own emotions.[42]

Fan Fiction in the Classroom

With the growing popularity of anime and manga, educators are beginning to unleash the power of fan fiction in their classrooms. English and composition teachers find that students are much more motivated to write when they are asked to create fan fiction. "It's really clear that if you have a genuine interest and a personal identification with the topic that you're learning about, your learning is going to be more engaging and, as a result, more successful,"[43] says Katie Davis. Not only do anime and manga fans enjoy engaging with their favorite characters or series as part of their schoolwork, they also find they have more to say than they might on other topics. "Even if you aren't the best writer, you might know everything there is to know about a certain character in the series,"[44] says Rebecca Black, a professor at the University of California, Irvine, who has studied fan fiction. When teachers pair up the students' enthusiasm and knowledge base, the results can be gratifying for students and teachers alike. "The authors whom we interviewed unanimously and unequivocally communicated their belief that fanfiction had helped them hone their craft,"[45] researchers Aragon and Davis write in their book, *Writers in the Secret Garden*.

The Perils of Shipping

The feelings anime and manga fans have for their favorite characters can run deep. These feelings can morph into hostility when a fan encounters someone who criticizes the character or ships him or her in a way the fan does not like. The result, says A.J Riley, a fan fiction author and a contributor to Medium, is that "fandoms can become a dark, toxic place" when fans dare to pair characters who are enemies or explore homoerotic relationships not established in the canon of the narrative. She explains:

> A lot of shippers who ship a canon ship hold almost a strong superiority complex over shippers who ship a non-canon ship. Especially if the non-canon ship . . . is a queer ship and the canon ship is a man and woman. And from my own experience, a lot of shippers of the canon ship will often mock and invalidate shippers of the popular non-canon ship and make them feel bad about shipping two men or two women and at times they will put other fans down for the things they do with their ships in terms of fan creativity (fan art, fanfiction, fan edits, manips [manipulations]). . . . Homophobia is often a strong thing in many fandoms.

A.J Riley, "The Dark Side of Fandom," Medium, July 27, 2023. https://ajrileyarticles.medium.com.

Anime and manga are primarily visual media, and fan art is an important component of fan culture. Fan artists also create new storylines for well-known characters. "As we follow along with the main characters it is hard not to be inspired by their determination and want to start drawing your own works,"[46] says fan artist and anime critic Magnolia. Illustrator Cochet Volaille says that the feelings stirred by a good character and story can be so overwhelming that a fan who loves drawing has no choice but to try to express themselves in their art. Volaille explains, "Sometimes shows and movies and comics thrill us so much and we have all this stuff we love about it fluttering around in our heads but no

> "As we follow along with the main characters it is hard not to be inspired by their determination and want to start drawing your own works."[46]
>
> —Magnolia, anime artist and critic

words seem to pull together into actual sentences. So you put that energy into drawing to show your appreciation and love for something."[47]

Fan artists can cast their favorite characters into new settings and challenge them to overcome new obstacles. They not only create original situations, they can also experiment with character expressions, actions, and costumes. Unconstrained by commercial requirements, fan artists move beyond traditional pencil, ink, and watercolor art into digital art, using programs like Photoshop and Procreate, and even into paintings, sculptures, and mixed media. Fan artists can showcase their work online on platforms such as Instagram; DeviantArt, a long-standing platform for artists to share and discover art; and microblogging sites like Tumblr.

Fan art is not limited to storytelling through two-dimensional drawing and painting. Musically inclined fans create original songs and soundtracks that they can pair with existing anime and manga art to create anime music videos and even full scores. Actors and voice talents often give dramatic readings of manga books in audiobooks and podcasts. All these platforms and forms of individual expression allow for user engagement and feedback, strengthening the bonds that hold the fan culture together.

CHAPTER FOUR

The Otaku Lifestyle

Expressing an interest in, respect for, and bond with a popular form of entertainment is a time-honored tradition that goes back at least one hundred years with the hero worship of figures like baseball player Babe Ruth, movie star Charlie Chaplin, and cartoon character Mickey Mouse. Fans often surround themselves with mementos of their idols—such as collectible cards, dolls, posters, and clothing. For example, sports fans often wear their favorite team's jerseys to show their loyalty to the franchise or to certain players. The consumer data company Statista reports that in 2024, the sales of sports jerseys in the United States surpassed $14 billion. Fans of anime and manga are no different, but their ranks among Americans aged twelve to twenty-five are even larger than those of the three largest professional sports. According to a 2022 survey by the Japanese public relations company Dentsu, 37.9 percent of American Gen Z survey respondents said they like action anime, 35.6 percent like family anime, and 34.3 percent like heroine anime. When asked about their interest in professional football, basketball, baseball, the percentages were lower—ranging from 30.2 percent to 21.7 percent.

In their survey, the Dentsu researchers asked their Gen Z sample group whether they considered themselves to be an otaku. The term *otaku* was coined in 1983 by humorist and editor Akio Nakamori to describe people with consuming interests, particularly in manga, anime, video games, or computers, often to the detriment of their social skills. Nakamori applied the term not only to fans of anime and manga but also to science-fiction fans and those who idolize pop stars.

According to a recent survey, more American Gen Z respondents said they like anime more than they did professional football, basketball, or baseball.

As the popularity of anime and manga spread around the world, the word *otaku* began to lose its negative connotations, especially outside Japan. Being known as an otaku became a badge of honor for many anime and manga fans. Now it is an affectionate term for people outside Japan who love Japanese products, art forms, and culture. In the Dentsu survey, 34 percent of respondents identified as an otaku. The researchers were taken aback. "In other words, an astounding 34% of America's Gen Z, or around 15 million people, acknowledge themselves as anime otaku. Amazing, isn't it?"[48]

Like sports fans, anime and manga fans like to show their solidarity in their favorite pastime. Otakus often express their enthusiasm for their favorite characters and series in their entire lifestyle—what they wear, how they decorate their room or home, and sometimes even how they customize their cars. "I am a girl, I love anime, and I am not ashamed of it," says Taylor Hall, a student at the University of Connecticut. "Being an Otaku is a part of who I am."[49]

A Massive Market

Commercial entities are happy to satisfy the customer demands of anime and manga fans, creating an endless stream of anime- and manga-related products, including clothing, jewelry, posters, figures, backpacks, notebooks, stickers, and decals. This, in turn, feeds more consumer demand. When fans of one character or series see a product featuring another, they often want the same item for themselves but emblazoned with their preferred manga or anime artwork.

Because of the fragmentation of the anime and manga worlds into various categories, it might seem impossible for manufacturers to satisfy such diverse demand. After all, there are hundreds of popular characters and series. It might seem unlikely that each one would have enough followers to create a viable market for anime- and manga-themed merchandise. Thanks to the internet, however, fans around the world can search for and find items from any supplier, no matter how small or specialized. Stephen Reysen, a professor in the Department of Psychology and Special Education at East Texas A&M University, writes:

> "I am a girl, I love anime, and I am not ashamed of it. . . . Being an Otaku is a part of who I am."[49]
>
> —Taylor Hall, student at the University of Connecticut

> New digital technology facilitated online shopping for anime, especially as it became more common for teens and young adults to have their own computers and access to

the internet, allowing them to watch their shows without needing to put them on the family television. . . . Technology also increased the ease with which fans could digitally download anime and contributed to the makers' profit margins.[50]

Another reason niche products can be successful is that the overall anime and manga market is huge. Konvoy Ventures, a gaming venture capital firm, reports that there are about 600 million anime and manga fans outside of China. Crunchyroll estimates that there were more than 800 million anime and manga fans globally by 2025. Since Crunchyroll excludes China and Japan from its estimate, the actual number of anime and manga fans is likely to be more than 1 billion people by 2025. Because anime and manga are visual media, the related products are not restricted by language. Konvoy Ventures estimated that the global anime market was $31 billion in 2024 and would grow to $44 billion by 2027. In such a huge marketplace, the makers of niche

The global anime market is expected to grow to $44 billion by 2027. In such a huge marketplace, niche anime products like action figures can still find enough buyers to make their production viable.

anime and manga products can still find enough buyers to make the production and marketing of such products viable.

A large part of the global anime market is made up of electronics. Thousands of anime and manga video games are available for consoles and cell phones. In addition, otakus can buy a wide range of apps and accessories for their phones, including anime watching apps, wallpaper apps, manga reading apps, and even posters and figures that come to life through smartphone apps via augmented reality (AR). Anime and manga apps allow otakus anywhere in the world to receive the latest releases as soon as they are available in Japan. Electronic tie-ins will continue to grow as virtual reality (VR) and AR platforms become more widespread. VR and AR are transforming anime and manga experiences. In a medium known as immersive storytelling, VR and AR will allow fans to interact with their favorite characters in simulated three-dimensional worlds.

Fast-Food Tie-Ins

Knowing the size of the market and the enthusiasm of the otaku consumers, big brands often partner with anime and manga creators to offer promotional tie-ins with much anticipated releases of movies, books, and television series. The tie-ins can range from fashion gear to toys and collectibles. One of the most innovative tie-ins occurred in February 2024, when McDonald's launched a mini anime series, a customized menu, and special packaging as part of its global campaign to appeal to anime and manga fans. The restaurant chain even flipped its iconic logo upside down, rebranding itself as WcDonald's. The special menu offered a ten-piece WcNuggets meal and Savory Chili WcDonald's sauce, with packaging designed by Japanese manga artist Acky Bright. Bright also created a weekly digital manga series that customers could access by scanning the QR code on the packaging. McDonald's also partnered with Japanese animation house studio Pierrot to produce four WcDonald's anime shorts, which fans in thirty countries could access online by scanning the code on the WcDonald's bag.

What is unusual is that the WcDonald's concept originated within anime and manga, not within the fast-food giant itself. WcDonald's first appeared in a 1983 Japanese anime episode titled "A Mystery for a Winter Night," which was part of a series based on the 1981 manga and anime franchise *Cat's Eye*. Even though the single letter *M* was rendered as a *W*, its yellow color on a red background immediately evoked the McDonald's logo. In 1985 the golden *W* appeared on a red package of French fries in the video game *Bubble Bobble*. The inverted logo was paired with the full name WacDonald's for the first time in a 1988 anime episode of *Aim for the Ace!* For four decades WcDonald's has appeared in cityscapes and restaurant scenes throughout different anime, manga, and video games. "The WcDonald's universe is a reflection of what fans have created," says Tariq Hassan, chief marketing and customer experience officer at McDonald's USA. "It honors their vision and celebrates their creativity, while authentically bringing it to life in our restaurants for the first time ever."[51]

When McDonald's brought in Bright to develop the WcDonald's characters and storylines, the artist knew that his job was not to create something entirely new, but rather to leverage the fictional restaurant chain's existing popularity among anime and manga fans. "I had a great time partnering with McDonald's to help make WcDonald's a reality for manga fans who have a genuine love for the brand," says Bright. "From the details of the diverse Crew characters to the manga plot itself, I loved being able to use my artwork to bring to life the dynamic, vibrant world of WcDonald's for people around the world."[52]

WcDonald's was not McDonald's first foray into anime promotions. It had already featured several anime-based toys in its Happy Meal promotions, including *Astro Boy*, *Yu-Gi-Oh!*, *Bakugan*, and *Pokémon*. Meanwhile, Burger King launched promotions featuring *Hamtaro*, *Pokémon*, and *Beyblade*. Both Taco Bell and Carl's Jr. had promotional tie-ins with *Cardcaptors*, an anime

The Impact of Anime on an Athlete's Life

An anonymous contributor to the *My Anime Story* blog tells how anime has provided him with inspiration to become a better sports competitor.

> Anime isn't just a form of entertainment; it's a source of inspiration that has enriched my life as a sports player. . . .
>
> The story of Naruto Uzumaki, a young ninja determined to become the Hokage, struck a chord with me. His undying spirit and relentless determination taught me the value of pushing beyond my limits on the field. When I face a tough opponent or a challenging practice session, Naruto's unwavering spirit reminds me to never give up, no matter the odds. This determination has made me a more resilient and committed sports player. . . .
>
> Anime often immerses us in surreal worlds, but it also teaches us the power of focus and visualization. Characters like Saitama from *One Punch Man* and Takumi Fujiwara from *Initial D* demonstrate unwavering focus on their goals. Their dedication to mastering their skills has inspired me to set clear objectives in sports and visualize my success.
>
> Before a game, I take a moment to mentally rehearse my moves and imagine myself excelling. This newfound mental preparation has boosted my confidence and performance in a range of sports.

Anonymous, "How My Passion for Anime Transformed My Journey as a Sports Player," *My Anime Story* (blog), October 22, 2023. https://myanimestory.org.

series that aired on Kids' WB. Taco Bell also had a multiyear promotion of *Digimon* collectible cards and toys. One of the more distinctive Taco Bell collectibles were the *Digimon* collector cels—translucent cards that allow light to shine through them like movie film. The cels featured still frames from *Digimon: The Movie*.

Anime Cafés

Fast-food chains are not the only restaurants catering to otaku diners. Anime-themed cafés have long been a staple in Japan and are now popping up all around the world. Pokémon Cafe in Tokyo is one of the best-known anime-theme restaurants. Opened in 2018, Pokémon Cafe not only is decorated with scenes from the anime series, it also offers menu items shaped and colored like the popular pocket monsters, including the Pikachu hamburger, Eevee plate, and Jigglypuff-shaped cheesecake. When it comes to cute, however, Tokyo's Kirby Café is second to none. It features service settings depicting the adorable anime food lover as well as burgers, pancakes, and a strawberry mousse modeled in his likeness. Guests even get a souvenir Kirby plate to take home when they order the burger and meat pasta combo. Rather than sticking with one popular series, two Tokyo cafés—Charaum Cafe and Animate Cafe Ikebukuro—collaborate with anime developers to create themes that have a limited run. For example, Charaum teamed up with *Attack on Titan* and *YuYu Hakusho*, and Animate Cafe Ikebukuro showcased *My Hero Academia*.

Pokémon Cafe in Tokyo is one of the best-known anime-themed restaurants. Opened in 2018, it offers items on the menu shaped and colored like the popular pocket monsters.

The anime café concept has spread to the United States as well. In 2024 a *One Piece*–themed restaurant opened in Las Vegas. The first US anime restaurant with a licensed tie-in with a series, One Piece Cafe offers a menu featuring Sanji's seafood friend rice, Tajio's beef curry, the Franky burger and fries, and a Might Meats Pirate Platter that features the restaurant's version of Luffy's iconic meat-on-the-bone. Meals are served in colorful cardboard boxes with illustrations from the series, including drawings of Monkey D. Luffy, Vinsmoke Sanji, and Franky.

"We feel that by blending the love of anime and food, we've created more than just a restaurant. We've created a hub for cultural exchange and community connection."[53]

—Joy Nguyen, co-owner of anime café Soupa Saiyan

Other American anime-themed restaurants include *Naruto*-themed Silverlake Ramen in Los Angeles; multiple anime series–themed Rayaki, with locations in New Jersey and Pennsylvania; the Dragon Bowl C Noodle Bar, a *Dragon Ball*–themed ramen bar in Conroe, Texas; and Soupa Saiyan, three *Dragon Ball Z*–themed noodle restaurants in Orlando, Florida. The name Soupa Saiyan is a pun on Super Saiyan, the immensely powerful alien characters in *Dragon Ball Z*. The owners, Joy and Marshall Nguyen, say they founded their restaurants to give anime fans a place to feel comfortable. Joy explains that her husband felt judged for being an otaku when he was younger. She says:

> Growing up, he always felt like kids (made) fun of him or (thought) he's weird, so he (felt) like all the other anime fans out there must feel the same. So opening Soupa Saiyan, he knows that this is dedicated to them. They can feel good enjoying a bowl of noodles with their kind of people without feeling judged. . . . We feel that by blending the love of anime and food, we've created more than just a restaurant. We've created a hub for cultural exchange and community connection.[53]

Anime and Manga Designs at Home

Anime and manga fans do not always have the time or budget to seek out an anime-themed restaurant, but they can always make a steaming hot bowl of anime-inspired ramen noodles at home or feast on any number of snacks with tie-ins to popular series. For example, ramen maker Ichiraku offers five kinds of packaged ramen—miso, chicken, beef, beef curry, and seafood—with packaging featuring characters from the popular series *Naruto*. Packaged soups with anime tie-ins are also popular. Marumiya Foods offers a *Kimetsu no Yaiba* mild curry pork and corn soup, and Prince Katsu has three soups featuring *Hello Kitty* anime packaging: Kuromi spicy beef pho noodle soup cup, My Melody chicken lemongrass pho noodle soup, and Hello Kitty chicken noodle soup. For fans who want to season their own ramen noodles, Surreal Entertainment markets a One Piece Sanji Shichimi Togarashi spicy ramen seasoning powder. For dessert, there is a range of candies, including Naruto Gummy Ramen.

Once at home, the otaku can curl up with all kinds of anime- and manga-inspired home decor items—pillows, comforters, blankets, and sheets. One item growing in popularity is the *dakimakura*—a body-length pillow from Japan that is usually coupled with pillow covers depicting anime characters."

Anime and manga posters, lamps, and figures can liven up an otaku's living space. For a dramatic effect, online sellers Amazon, Temu, and even Walmart offer wall-sized tapestries depicting scenes from popular anime and manga series, including *Bleach*, *One Piece*, *Naruto*, Studio Ghibli's *Spirited Away*, and *Jujutsu Kaisen*. The print-on-demand company Anime Ape offers more than 150 different anime and manga wall tapestries along with a mind-boggling array of themed wearables, including shirts, sweaters, hoodies, shorts, tights, and even underwear. The company features designs from more than two hundred anime and manga series—from *Ace of Diamond* to *Zoids*. For fans who want something not shown on the website, Anime Ape states that customers can contact it to request a new design.

Saved by Anime

Taylor Hall, a student at the University of Connecticut, watched *Pokémon* as a child and then, at age eleven, became a fan of *Sailor Moon*. Her love of anime grew throughout her teen years, but in high school, she began to be bullied. "One of the reasons was because of my love of anime," she recalls. "People called me a freak, a weirdo, etc. My whole freshman year I had no friends and spent almost every day crying." Hall gave up talking about anime or even watching it. She spiraled into depression. Then one day she was browsing on her computer and came across the show *Naruto*. The main character had no friends and was shunned by his village, but he never lost his fighting spirit. The story resonated with Hall, who says, "Watching *Naruto* really changed my life. It brought me out of my depression and gave me a fire to keep living. If Naruto could keep fighting, then why can't I? I shouldn't let people's words make me feel worthless. . . . This anime show is more than just a show. It inspires me to never give up, to keep fighting and keep my head up. . . . Anime . . . saved my life."

Taylor Hall, "I Am a Girl, I Love Anime, and I Am Not Ashamed of It," Odyssey, July 2, 2018. www.theodysseyonline.com.

Anime Art on Wheels

One of the most eye-catching displays of personal fandom and creativity are Dekocars—automobiles enveloped by oversized decals depicting scenes from manga and anime. Ken Miyoshi, the producer of the Dekocar Showoff that is part of the Nisei Week, a Japanese cultural festival held annually in the Little Tokyo area of Los Angeles, explains:

> "Dekocar" is coined from a new term by shortening "decoration car"—the closest genre would be "Itasha" from Japan, but [as] with anything that hits America, this country adds their own flair. It's sort of similar to what happened to sushi. The pure form of sushi came from Japan to the States, but then we add something new, as new types of sushi were born like the California roll, Volcano roll, etc.[54]

Most Dekocars are Japanese brands, like Honda and Toyota, but any car or even motorcycle can be themed out with the anime wraps. One of the highlights of the Dekocar Showoff was a Porsche customized with a body kit and covered with dramatic artwork from the *Mobile Suit Gundam Thunderbolt* manga series. Each Dekocar is custom made. "Upgrades like body kits are visual but mostly made in many quantities and model specific," says Miyoshi. "With Dekocar, the owners can design, print, and install these on various models but still create a full on 'one-off' design upgrade."[55]

"At its core, the Dekocar Showoff embodies the marriage of Japanese and American cultures."[56]

—Andrew Beckford, writer for *Motor Trend*

The themed decoration of Dekocars can extend to the interior as well. Fans sometimes add anime- and manga-themed figurines, toys, plushies, and pillows to the interiors of their cars to match their Dekocar designs. One Dekocar pickup truck at the Nisei Week show had its bed filled with colorful plastic balls to make a ball pit for various anime and manga plushies. "At its core, the Dekocar Showoff embodies the marriage of Japanese and American cultures, which is essentially part of what Downtown LA's annual Nisei Festival is all about,"[56] says Andrew Beckford, a writer for *Motor Trend* magazine.

The marriage of Japanese and American culture is also what being an otaku is all about. It is not limited to enjoying anime and manga stories alone. It encompasses many aspects of Japanese culture—from food and fashion to art and decor. It also embraces the themes of anime and manga: love, respect, loyalty, bravery, and strength. Being an otaku is not a fad. It is a lifestyle that adds purpose and meaning to the lives of individuals facing the challenges of the modern world.

SOURCE NOTES

Introduction: A Deep Connection

1. Giacco Danielle, "Fandom Unleashed: Exploring the Unique Subcultures of Anime," Medium, November 2, 2023. https://medium.com.
2. Hacker-chan, email interview with the author, November 18, 2024.
3. Rachael Lefler, "Why Do People Get So Obsessed with Anime?," HubPages, March 28, 2023. https://discover.hubpages.com.

Chapter One: Sharing a Passion

4. Christian Markle, "From Reddit to MyAnimeList, Why Anime Fans Need Online Discussions," CBR, July 26, 2023. www.cbr.com.
5. Markle, "From Reddit to MyAnimeList, Why Anime Fans Need Online Discussions."
6. Melissa Ojeda, "10 Harsh Realities of Being a *My Hero Academia* Fan," CBR, June 3, 2022. www.cbr.com.
7. A.J. Riley, "The Dark Side of Fandom," Medium, July 27, 2023. https://ajrileyarticles.medium.com.
8. Quoted in Fritz Lalley, "Thriving Anime Club Reflects Nationwide Trend," Amherst Student, March 1, 2023. https://amherststudent.com.
9. Lalley, "Thriving Anime Club Reflects Nationwide Trend."
10. Iyashikei, "The Role of Modern Anime," Medium, October 3, 2017. https://medium.com.
11. Danielle, "Fandom Unleashed."
12. Moonbear Tsukino, "Kagero Sketch from Yusuke Kozaki!!!," Amino, July 7, 2019. https://aminoapps.com.
13. Quoted in IMDb, "Kunal Nayyar Quotes." www.imdb.com.
14. Quoted in Philiana Ng, "Chris Hardwick Reveals Details of BBC America Deal, How Nerdist Podcast Will Be Adapted for TV (Q&A)," *Hollywood Reporter*, May 25, 2011. www.hollywoodreporter.com.
15. Quoted in John Gaudiosi, "The Queen of Comic-Con, Felicia Day, Talks Games, Tech and Geek and Sundry," *Forbes*, July 12, 2012. www.forbes.com.
16. Trey Bates, "The Rise of Anime and Manga in Japan: A Cultural Shift That Has Captivated the World," Medium, April 8, 2023. https://medium.com.

Chapter Two: The World of Cosplay

17. Quoted in Ayako Nakano, "Japan's Innovative Performance Wins at World Cosplay Summit ESG/SDGs," *Japan Times* (Tokyo), August 30, 2024. https://sustainable.japantimes.com.
18. Admin, "Some Cosplay Ideas That Are Popular and Relevant for 2023," *Anime Costume Blog*, February 10, 2023. www.animecustome.com.

19. Quoted in Osmud Rahman et al., "'Cosplay': Imaginative Self and Performing Identity," *Fashion Theory*, September 2012. www.researchgate.net.
20. Quoted in Safa Warsi and Robert T. Muller, "Becoming Another Person Through Cosplay," *Talking About Trauma* (blog), *Psychology Today*, December 2, 2021. www.psychologytoday.com.
21. Quoted in Amanda Ellard, "When Escaping Reality Helps Define Identity: Expression and Empowerment in the Cosplay Community," *Smithsonian*, September 8, 2023. https://folklife.si.edu.
22. Quoted in Ellard, "When Escaping Reality Helps Define Identity."
23. Quoted in Ashley Lotecki, "Cosplay Culture: The Development of Interactive and Living Art Through Play," Toronto Metropolitan University, May 24, 2021. https://rshare.library.torontomu.ca.
24. Quoted in Lotecki, "Cosplay Culture."
25. Quoted in Cosplay.com, "Accuracy vs Feeling Comfortable." https://cosplay.com.
26. Quoted in Cosplay.com, "Accuracy vs Feeling Comfortable."
27. Knockabout, "Cosplayers—Do You Make Adjustments for Comfort?," Reddit, April 15, 2024. www.reddit.com.
28. Quoted in Rahman et al., "'Cosplay.'"
29. Quoted in Rahman et al., "'Cosplay.'"
30. Rahman et al., "'Cosplay.'"
31. Quoted in Warsi and Muller, "Becoming Another Person Through Cosplay."

Chapter Three: Artistic Endeavors

32. KK Miller, "Fabulous Ghibli Fan Art Inspires Us All to Pick Up a Pencil and Get Drawing," Sora News 24, September 19, 2015. https://soranews24.com.
33. Lefler, "Why Do People Get So Obsessed with Anime?"
34. Lefler, "Why Do People Get So Obsessed with Anime?"
35. Quoted in Sourojit Ghosh and Cecilia Aragon, "Leveraging Community Support and Platform Affordances on a Path to More Active Participation: A Study of Online Fan Fiction Communities," Transformative Works and Cultures, March 14, 2024. https://journal.transformativeworks.org.
36. Quoted in Ghosh and Aragon, "Leveraging Community Support and Platform Affordances on a Path to More Active Participation."
37. Quoted in Ghosh and Aragon, "Leveraging Community Support and Platform Affordances on a Path to More Active Participation."
38. Quoted in Ghosh and Aragon, "Leveraging Community Support and Platform Affordances on a Path to More Active Participation."
39. Ghosh and Aragon, "Leveraging Community Support and Platform Affordances on a Path to More Active Participation."
40. Quoted in Julie Beck, "What Fan Fiction Teaches That the Classroom Doesn't," *Atlantic*, October 1, 2019. www.theatlantic.com.
41. Effie Sapuridis, "Expert Insight: There's So Much More to 'Shipping' than Wanting Characters to Kiss," Western News, October 3, 2024. https://news.westernu.ca.

42. Sapuridis, "Expert Insight."
43. Quoted in Beck, "What Fan Fiction Teaches That the Classroom Doesn't."
44. Quoted in Beck, "What Fan Fiction Teaches That the Classroom Doesn't."
45. Cecilia Aragon and Katie Davis, *Writers in the Secret Garden*. Cambridge, MA: MIT Press, 2019, p. 60.
46. Magnolia, "10 Inspiring Anime for Artists and Art Lovers Alike," UnVale, January 6, 2023. https://blog.unvale.io.
47. Quoted in Quora, "Why Do I Like Drawing Fanart So Much?," 2019. www.quora.com.

Chapter Four: The Otaku Lifestyle

48. Eimi Shimizu, "The Numbers Speak for Themselves! Anime Is Killer Content for Gen Z," Dentsu Inc., December 4, 2023. www.dentsu.co.jp.
49. Taylor Hall, "I Am a Girl, I Love Anime, and I Am Not Ashamed of It," Odyssey, July 2, 2018. www.theodysseyonline.com.
50. Stephen Reysen et al., *Transported to Another World, The Psychology of Anime Fans*. Commerce, TX: International Anime Research Project, 2021, p. 2.
51. Quoted in McDonald's Corporation, "Welcome to WcDonald's: McDonald's Brings Anime Fans' Favorite Fictional Restaurant to Life," February 21, 2024. https://corporate.mcdonalds.com.
52. Quoted in McDonald's Corporation, "Welcome to WcDonald's."
53. Quoted in Brooke Savage, "Orlando's *Dragon Ball Z*–Themed Restaurants Serve Noodles, Culture and Community," News 6, May 18, 2023. www.clickorlando.com.
54. Quoted in Andrew Beckford, "Nisei Week Dekocar Show 2019," *Motor Trend*, August 22, 2019. www.motortrend.com.
55. Quoted in Beckford, "Nisei Week Dekocar Show 2019."
56. Quoted in Beckford, "Nisei Week Dekocar Show 2019."

FOR FURTHER RESEARCH

Books

Cecilia Aragon and Katie Davis, *Writers in the Secret Garden*. Cambridge, MA: MIT Press, 2019.

Jonathan Clements, *Anime: A History*. 2nd ed. London: British Film Institute, 2023.

Robert Henderson, *Quick Guide to Anime and Manga*. San Diego, CA: ReferencePoint, 2022.

Brigitte Koyama-Richard, *One Thousand Years of Manga*. London: Thames & Hudson, 2022.

Remi Lopez, *The Impact of Akira: A Manga (R)evolution*. Toulouse, France: Third Editions, 2021.

Bradley Steffens, *The Rise of Anime and Manga*. San Diego, CA: ReferencePoint, 2023.

Internet Sources

Matija Ferjan, "20+ Anime Statistics & Facts: How Many People Watch Anime? (2024)." Headphones Addict, January 8, 2024. https://headphonesaddict.com.

Will Heath, "20 Best Female Manga Artists You Need to Know," Japan Objects, October 9, 2020. https://japanobjects.com.

IGN Staff, "25 Best Anime of All Time," Japan Web Magazine, August 30, 2023. www.ign.com.

Interac Network, "Otaku Culture in Japan—Japanese Anime, Manga, Idols & Video Games," November 24, 2021. https://interacnetwork.com.

Okuha, "The Best Anime Artists of All Time," March 8, 2023. https://okuha.com.

Websites

Anime News Network
www.animenewsnetwork.com
This website provides news, reviews, and feature reports on anime, manga, and video games, as well as brief bios of manga and anime artists.

Cosplay Advice
https://cosplayadvice.com
This fan-made site offers tips and photos for making safe and realistic cosplay costumes and props.

GKIDS
https://gkids.com
This is the official website of GKIDS, the producer and distributor of animated movies. Visitors can find information about previous releases, including synopses and sample art from each film. The website also has a blog with interviews of various anime artists and news about upcoming releases.

Iyashikei
https://iyashikei.moe
Iyashikei, Japanese for "healing," is an otaku lifestyle blog, dedicated to celebrating otaku culture and the media it surrounds.

Tezuka Osamu Official Website
https://tezukaosamu.net/en
This site is a collection of items related to the late manga artist Tezuka Osamu, including a profile, a timeline of his life, photo albums, an animated short about his life (in Japanese only), and the wisdom he wanted to pass on to future generations in his "Message for Earth."

T.H.E.M. Anime Reviews
www.themanime.org
This website offers up-to-date reviews of anime in all forms, including movies, television, and direct-to-video releases. It includes a huge, searchable archive of past reviews, arranged in alphabetical order by title. It also hosts message boards on a wide range of topics.

TV Tropes
https://tvtropes.org
This website is a wiki—edited and managed by its own audience, using a web browser. It includes entries on all aspects of popular culture, including manga and anime.

INDEX

PICTURE CREDITS

Cover: kahiko0147/Shutterstock

6: REDXII/Shutterstock
9: Sharaf Maksumov/Shutterstock
12: Colleen Michaels/Shutterstock
16: Nick Starichenko/Shutterstock
21: Radheya Photos/Shutterstock
25: ANTONIOCR/Shutterstock
28: CTK/Alamy Stock Photo
33: MarbellaStudio/Shutterstock
35: Emre Akkoyun/Shutterstock
39: Entertainment Pictures/Alamy Stock Photo
44: Howard Weiss/Shutterstock
46: Antonello Marangi/Shutterstock
50: Hannari_eli/Shutterstock

ABOUT THE AUTHOR

Bradley Steffens is a novelist, poet, and award-winning author of more than seventy nonfiction books for children and young adults.